THIS JOURNAL BELONGS TO

START DATE

/   /

SHE READS TRUTH™

© 2019 She Reads Truth, LLC
All rights reserved.

ISBN 978-1-949526-53-0

No part of this publication may be reproduced, distributed, or transmitted in any form or by any means, including photocopying, recording, or other electronic or mechanical methods, without the prior written permission of She Reads Truth, LLC, except in the case of brief quotations embodied in critical reviews and certain other noncommercial uses permitted by copyright law.

All Scripture is taken from the Christian Standard Bible®, Copyright © 2017 by Holman Bible Publishers. Used by permission. Christian Standard Bible® and CSB® are federally registered trademarks of Holman Bible Publishers.

BIBLE STUDY JOURNAL

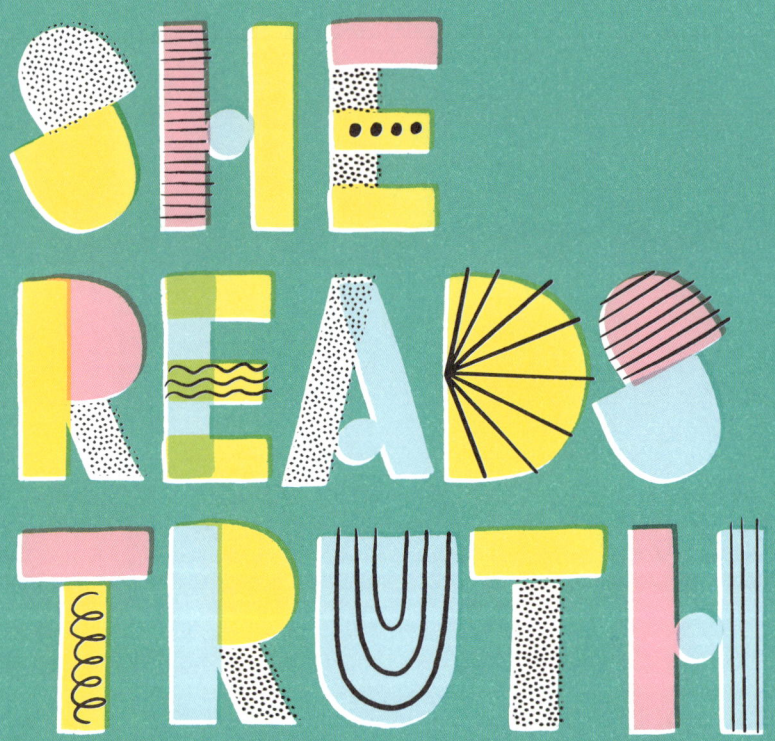

BUT THESE ARE WRITTEN SO THAT YOU MAY BELIEVE THAT JESUS IS THE MESSIAH, THE SON OF GOD, AND THAT BY BELIEVING YOU MAY HAVE LIFE IN HIS NAME.

John 20:31

✳ THE BIBLE IS THE WORD OF GOD.

2 Timothy 3:16–17

✳ THE BIBLE WILL LAST FOREVER.

Isaiah 40:8

✳ THE BIBLE IS TRUE AND COMPLETE.

Revelation 22:6

✳ THE BIBLE CHANGES THE WAY WE LIVE.

James 1:22

✳ THE BIBLE IS FOR YOU.

Luke 11:28

YOUR WORD IS A LAMP FOR MY FEET
AND A LIGHT ON MY PATH.

Psalm 119:105

FACTS ABOUT ACTS

Acts is the **44th** book in the Bible.

Acts is the **5th** book in the New Testament.

LUKE wrote the book of Acts. He traveled with the apostle **PAUL**.

Acts tells the story of the **EARLY CHURCH** in the years following Jesus's resurrection.

Acts is the **SEQUEL** to the Gospel of Luke (also written by Luke).

Only three books in the Bible record Jesus's ascension into heaven. Acts is one of them!

There are **32** speeches in the book of Acts, most of them given by Peter and Paul.

Acts mostly follows Peter for the first 12 chapters, and Paul for last 16.

Acts is a book with lots of **TRAVEL**, including three missionary journeys and a boat trip to Rome!

In the book of Acts, God gives the Holy Spirit to His followers to fulfill Jesus's promise.

HOW TO USE THIS JOURNAL

Read one section of Acts at a time, using this journal to write down notes, questions, thoughts, and prayers as you read.

SHE READS
Open your Bible to read the Scripture.

FOCUS VERSES
Focus on these key verses to answer the study questions.

SHE STUDIES
Use this space to take notes as you read.

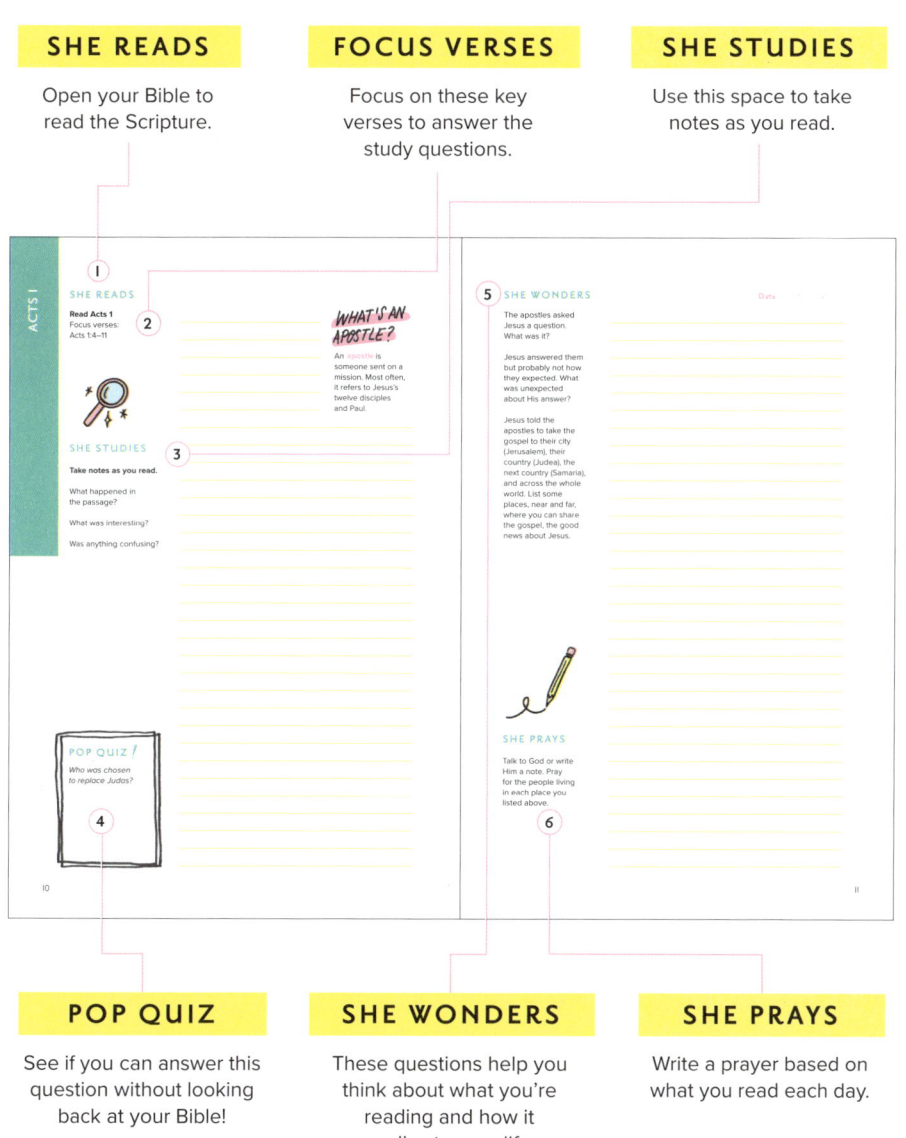

POP QUIZ
See if you can answer this question without looking back at your Bible!

SHE WONDERS
These questions help you think about what you're reading and how it applies to your life.

SHE PRAYS
Write a prayer based on what you read each day.

WHY 44?

Why is the number 44 on the cover of this journal?
Acts is the 44th book in the Bible.

#44 ACTS!

KEY VERSE

"BUT YOU WILL RECEIVE POWER WHEN THE HOLY SPIRIT HAS COME ON YOU, AND YOU WILL BE MY WITNESSES IN JERUSALEM, IN ALL JUDEA AND SAMARIA, AND TO THE END OF THE EARTH."

ACTS 1:8

ACTS 1

SHE READS

Read Acts 1
Focus verses:
Acts 1:4–11

SHE STUDIES

Take notes as you read.

What happened in the passage?

What was interesting?

Was anything confusing?

An **apostle** is someone sent on a mission. Most often, it refers to Jesus's twelve disciples and Paul.

POP QUIZ!

Who was chosen to replace Judas?

SHE WONDERS

Date   /   /

The apostles asked Jesus a question. What was it?

Jesus answered them but probably not how they expected. What was unexpected about His answer?

Jesus told the apostles to take the gospel to their city (Jerusalem), their country (Judea), the next country (Samaria), and across the whole world. List some places, near and far, where you can share the gospel, the good news about Jesus.

SHE PRAYS

Talk to God or write Him a note. Pray for the people living in each place you listed above.

11

ACTS 2

SHE READS

Read Acts 2
Focus verses:
Acts 2:1–21

SHE STUDIES

Take notes as you read.

What happened in the passage?

What was interesting?

Was anything confusing?

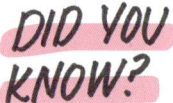

The Holy Spirit is mentioned more than forty times in the book of Acts.

POP QUIZ!

What time did Peter give his sermon?

SHE WONDERS

Date   /   /

Who came upon the people in Acts 2:4? What happened?

What does verse 8 reveal about God's plan for the spread of the gospel?

What promise is found in verse 21?

SHE PRAYS

Talk to God or write Him a note. Thank Him for the Holy Spirit.

ACTS 3

SHE READS

Read Acts 3
Focus verses:
Acts 3:11–26

SHE STUDIES

Take notes as you read.

What happened in the passage?

What was interesting?

Was anything confusing?

POP QUIZ!

Where was the lame man when he was healed?

SHE WONDERS

Date   /   /

Peter gives a lot of speeches in Acts, and this is his third one. Who is it for? What does he say about Jesus?

Reread verse 20. What do you think a "season of refreshing" from God is like? What did Peter say comes before a season of refreshing?

SHE PRAYS

Talk to God or write Him a note. Thank Him that we can repent and turn back to Him.

15

ACTS 4:1–22

SHE READS

Read Acts 4:1–22
Focus verses:
Acts 4:8–22

SHE STUDIES

Take notes as you read.

What happened in the passage?

What was interesting?

Was anything confusing?

POP QUIZ!

What group arrested Peter and John?

SHE WONDERS

Date   /   /

Copy verse 12.

Peter and John were really bold! What were they doing? Why were people so amazed?

Have you ever been really bold about your faith? What was it like? How did you feel?

SHE PRAYS

Talk to God or write Him a note. Ask Him to help you be bold in your faith.

SHE READS

Read Acts 4:23–36; Acts 5:1–11
Focus verses:
Acts 4:32–5:11

SHE STUDIES

Take notes as you read.

What happened in the passage?

What was interesting?

Was anything confusing?

POP QUIZ!

What does the name Barnabas mean?

SHE WONDERS

Date   /   /

Here we see two examples of people giving to the local church to care for those in need. What did Barnabas do?

Why were Ananias and Sapphira punished? Who did they lie to?

What does this story teach you about how God wants the church to care for others?

SHE PRAYS

Talk to God or write Him a note. Ask Him to show you ways you can give to your church or to those in need in your community.

ACTS 5:12–42

SHE READS

Read Acts 5:12–42
Focus verses:
Acts 5:25–42

SHE STUDIES

Take notes as you read.

What happened in the passage?

What was interesting?

Was anything confusing?

POP QUIZ!

Who convinced the Jewish leaders not to kill the apostles?

SHE WONDERS

Date   /   /

What did the Jewish council order the apostles not to do? How did the apostles respond?

Read verses 40–42 again. Why do you think Peter and the apostles kept preaching about Jesus?

How does the faith of the apostles inspire you?

SHE PRAYS

Talk to God or write Him a note. Thank Him for the faithfulness of the apostles and for offering us the same gift of faith.

ACTS 6

SHE READS

Read Acts 6
Focus verses:
Acts 6:1–7

SHE STUDIES

Take notes as you read.

What happened in the passage?

What was interesting?

Was anything confusing?

POP QUIZ!

How many men did the apostles pick to serve the widows?

SHE WONDERS

Date   /   /

What did the widows need? How did their church provide for them?

In what ways can you serve people in your church? If you're not sure, ask yourself: *Where is there a need? What gifts and talents has God given me? What do I enjoy doing?*

SHE PRAYS

Talk to God or write Him a note. Thank Him for the ways you can serve others by using the gifts He has given you.

ACTS 7:1–53

SHE READS

Read Acts 7:1–53
Focus verses:
Acts 7:9, 35, 39, 51

SHE STUDIES

Take notes as you read.

What happened in the passage?

What was interesting?

Was anything confusing?

POP QUIZ!

Moses fled and became a stranger in what land?

SHE WONDERS

Date   /   /

Look again at verses 9, 35, 39, and 51. What do you think Stephen was trying to explain to the Jewish leaders?

Stephen knew the leaders had the power to hurt him or even kill him, but he kept speaking the truth about Jesus! What do you think motivated him to do this?

SHE PRAYS

Talk to God or write Him a note about what you learned from today's reading.

ACTS 7:54–60; ACTS 8

SHE READS

Read Acts 7:54–60; Acts 8
Focus verses:
Acts 8:26–40

SHE STUDIES

Take notes as you read.

What happened in the passage?

What was interesting?

Was anything confusing?

POP QUIZ!

What was the name of the young man who witnessed Stephen's death?

SHE WONDERS

Date   /   /

The Ethiopian official was confused by what he was reading in Isaiah. Have you ever been confused when reading the Bible? Who in your life can you turn to for help when you have questions?

Because Philip listened to God, he was able to share the good news about Jesus with the official. What would you say if someone asked you about Jesus?

SHE PRAYS

Talk to God or write Him a note. Ask Him to prepare you for times when you can share the gospel.

ACTS 9:1-31

SHE READS

Read Acts 9:1–31
Focus verses:
Acts 9:20–31

SHE STUDIES

Take notes as you read.

What happened in the passage?

What was interesting?

Was anything confusing?

POP QUIZ!

How many days did Saul spend without his sight?

SHE WONDERS

Date   /   /

What an incredible transformation! How was Saul changed by God?

What obstacles did Saul face when he first started to share the good news about Jesus? How did God protect him?

Down through history, God has used many different people to spread this good news. How has God given you opportunities to share the gospel?

SHE PRAYS

Talk to God or write Him a note. Thank Him that the same gospel that changed Saul's life has been faithfully passed on, down through history, to you!

PEOPLE IN ACTS

There are a lot of people mentioned in the book of Acts. Here's a look at how some of them are connected.

THEOPHILUS
The book of Acts is dedicated to him. (So is the book of Luke!)
Acts 1:1

LUKE
Wrote Acts and likely interviewed Peter so he could write the Gospel of Luke. Traveled with Paul.
Acts 1:1; Luke 1:2; Colossians 4:14

JAMES
Jesus's half-brother who led the church in Jerusalem. Saw that God had changed Paul's heart and blessed his ministry to Gentiles (non-Jewish people).
Acts 12:1–2; Galatians 2:9

SIMON THE MAGICIAN
Samaritan who wanted to buy the ability to give the Holy Spirit to another person. (Peter said no.)
Acts 8:9–25

MATTHIAS
Chosen by the apostles to replace Judas Iscariot.
Acts 1:15–26

GAMALIEL
Member of the Jewish ruling council. Argued for letting Peter and the other apostles out of prison. Taught Paul about Scripture before Paul encountered Jesus.
Acts 5:34–35; Acts 22:3

CORNELIUS
Centurion (a Roman military leader) who invited Peter to his house. His whole family became followers of Jesus.
Acts 10:1–48

PETER
Apostle who told Jewish people about Jesus.
Acts 1:12–14; 2:14; 15:7

ANANIAS AND SAPPHIRA
Lied to God (and Peter) about their generosity and fell down dead.
Acts 5:1–11

DORCAS
Also known as Tabitha. Christian woman who died, but God used Peter to raise her back to life.
Acts 9:36–43

PHILIP
Deacon (servant-leader) in the church in Jerusalem. Led the Ethiopian official to faith.
Acts 6:1–7

STEPHEN
Deacon (servant-leader) in the Jerusalem church along with Philip. Killed for his faith in Jesus.
Acts 6:1–15

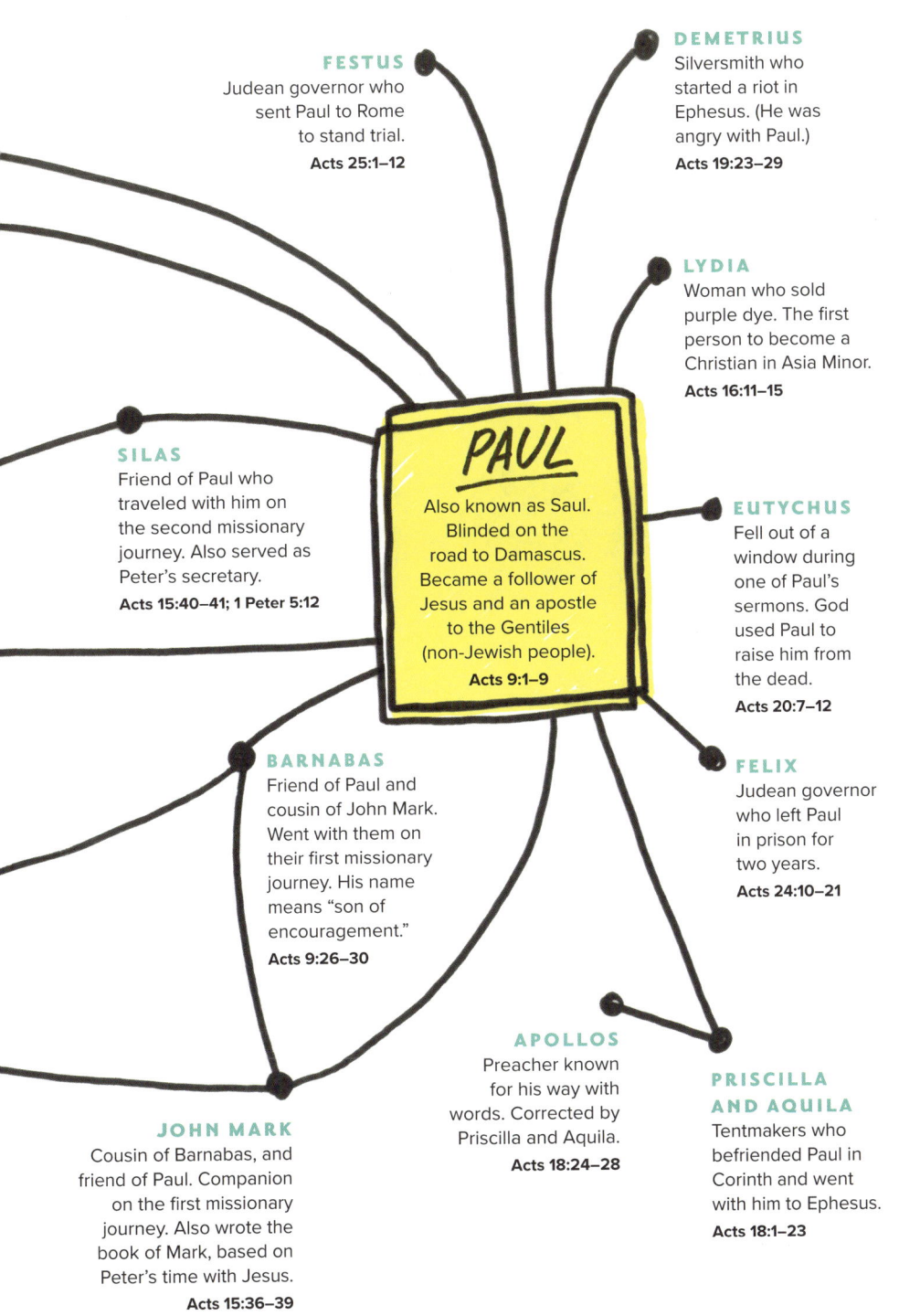

TEST YOUR KNOWLEDGE!

Complete the crossword puzzle. Look back at the chart on pages 30–31 if you need help.

*DOWN

 Led the Ethiopian official to faith in Jesus

 His name means "son of encouragement"

 The book of Acts is dedicated to him

 Apostle who told Jewish people about Jesus

 She and her husband were tentmakers who became friends of Paul

*ACROSS

 Chosen to replace Judas Iscariot

 Blinded on the road to Damascus

 Roman centurion who invited Peter to his house

 She sold purple dye and became a Christian in Philippi

 Christian woman who died, but God used Peter to raise her back to life

SHE READS

Read Acts 9:32–43
Focus verses:
Acts 9:32–43

SHE STUDIES

Take notes as you read.

What happened in the passage?

What was interesting?

Was anything confusing?

POP QUIZ!

Peter told Aeneas to get up and then do what?

SHE WONDERS

Date   /   /

Peter became known for his ability to heal people, but who was really doing the healing? Why do you think Peter made sure people knew that?

James 1:17 tells us all good gifts come from God. How can you give God the glory for the gifts He has given you?

SHE PRAYS

Talk to God or write Him a note. Name some good gifts in your life and thank God for them.

ACTS 10

SHE READS

Read Acts 10
Focus verses:
Acts 10:34–48

SHE STUDIES

Take notes as you read.

What happened in the passage?

What was interesting?

Was anything confusing?

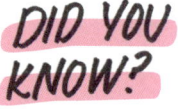

DID YOU KNOW?

In the Old Testament, God told His people to avoid eating certain animals, like pigs and lobsters. These animals were called "unclean," while animals that could be eaten were called "clean."

POP QUIZ !

How many times did Peter see the vision?

36

SHE WONDERS

Date / /

What changed for Peter over the course of today's reading? What did he realize about the gospel message and who it is for?

What happened when the Holy Spirit came down upon Cornelius's household (verse 44)?

Evangelism means sharing the gospel. How does knowing that the gospel is for everyone change the way you think about evangelism?

SHE PRAYS

Talk to God or write Him a note. Ask Him to show you what evangelism can look like in your everyday life.

ACTS 11

SHE READS

Read Acts 11
Focus verses:
Acts 11:19–26

SHE STUDIES

Take notes as you read.

What happened in the passage?

What was interesting?

Was anything confusing?

POP QUIZ!

Where did Barnabas go to find Saul?

SHE WONDERS

Date   /   /

How is Barnabas described in verse 24? What does he tell the new believers to do in verse 23?

What does it mean to be devoted to God?

Name a person in your life who encourages you in your faith.

SHE PRAYS

Talk to God or write Him a note. Ask Him to help you be devoted to Him.

ACTS 12

SHE READS

Read Acts 12
Focus verses:
Acts 12:1–19

SHE STUDIES

Take notes as you read.

What happened in the passage?

What was interesting?

Was anything confusing?

POP QUIZ!

What was the name of the servant girl?

SHE WONDERS

Date   /   /

How did the church respond to Peter being arrested? How did God answer?

What do you think it would have been like to hear that Peter was at the door?

God answered the prayers of the church! Think about a time you have prayed with other people for something. What did you learn?

SHE PRAYS

Talk to God or write Him a note. Thank Him for always hearing your prayers.

SHE READS

Read Acts 13
Focus verses:
Acts 13:42–52

SHE STUDIES

Take notes as you read.

What happened in the passage?

What was interesting?

Was anything confusing?

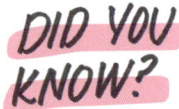

DID YOU KNOW?

A **Gentile** is anyone who is not Jewish. The book of Acts is about the spread of Jesus's message to both the Jewish people and the Gentiles.

POP QUIZ!

In this chapter, Luke starts calling Saul by a new name. What is it?

SHE WONDERS

Date   /   /

How did the Jewish leaders react to Paul's message?

Contrast the Jewish leaders' reaction with the reaction of the Gentiles.

Think back through what you've learned about the spread of the gospel in the book of Acts. What themes have you noticed? What have you learned about God?

SHE PRAYS

Talk to God or write Him a note. Thank Him for what He has taught you about Himself through the book of Acts so far.

SHE READS

Read Acts 14
Focus verses:
Acts 14:8–18

SHE STUDIES

Take notes as you read.

What happened in the passage?

What was interesting?

Was anything confusing?

POP QUIZ!

Whose temple was just outside Lystra?

SHE WONDERS

Date   /   /

Who did the people think Paul and Barnabas were? How did the crowd react?

Paul took this opportunity to tell the crowd about God. What truth about God did Paul explain in verse 15?

What are some areas in your life where you value other things more than God?

SHE PRAYS

Talk to God or write Him a note. Ask Him to show you anything you love more than Him and to help you always put Him first.

SHE READS

Read Acts 15:1–35
Focus verses:
Acts 15:1–21

SHE STUDIES

Take notes as you read.

What happened in the passage?

What was interesting?

Was anything confusing?

The Jerusalem Council represents a turning point in the early Church.

POP QUIZ!

Which apostle was the first to speak during the Jerusalem Council?

SHE WONDERS

Date   /   /

Some people said Gentiles should become Jewish in order to be true Christians. What did Peter say in response?

Look back in your Bible to Amos 9:11–12. When James quoted these verses to the council, what did he reveal about God's plan?

The apostles were constantly pointing back to the Old Testament as they told people about Jesus. Why do you think they did that?

SHE PRAYS

Talk to God or write Him a note. Thank Him for the gift of the Old Testament and how He works through His Word.

SHE READS

Read Acts 15:36–41; Acts 16:1–15
Focus verses:
Acts 16:11–15

SHE STUDIES

Take notes as you read.

What happened in the passage?

What was interesting?

Was anything confusing?

DID YOU KNOW?

Purple cloth was dyed using an extract from a type of sea snail. It was *very* expensive.

POP QUIZ!

Where was the man in Paul's vision from?

SHE WONDERS

Date   /   /

What happened to Lydia's heart in Acts 16:14?

God can use the words of other people to remind us of the good news, but ultimately it is God who opens our hearts. How can this change the way you pray for other people? For yourself?

SHE PRAYS

Talk to God or write Him a note. Make a list of people in your life who don't know Jesus and ask God to open their hearts.

SHE READS

Read Acts 16:16–40
Focus verses:
Acts 16:25–40

SHE STUDIES

Take notes as you read.

What happened in the passage?

What was interesting?

Was anything confusing?

POP QUIZ!

Paul and Silas were citizens of _____.

SHE WONDERS

Date   /   /

What surprised you about how Paul and Silas acted in prison?

How did God work through Paul and Silas's time in prison?

What does this story teach you about God? How can it change your perspective on your own difficult experiences?

SHE PRAYS

Talk to God or write Him a note. Thank Him for how He is always working, even in difficult times.

ACTS 17

SHE READS

Read Acts 17
Focus verses:
Acts 17:22–34

SHE STUDIES

Take notes as you read.

What happened in the passage?

What was interesting?

Was anything confusing?

POP QUIZ!

Where did Paul make his speech?

SHE WONDERS

Date   /   /

This is one of Paul's most famous speeches. What did he proclaim about God? Make a list.

What did Paul say people should do in response to God?

How can you respond to God based on what you read from Paul?

SHE PRAYS

Talk to God or write Him a note based on what you learned about Him in today's reading.

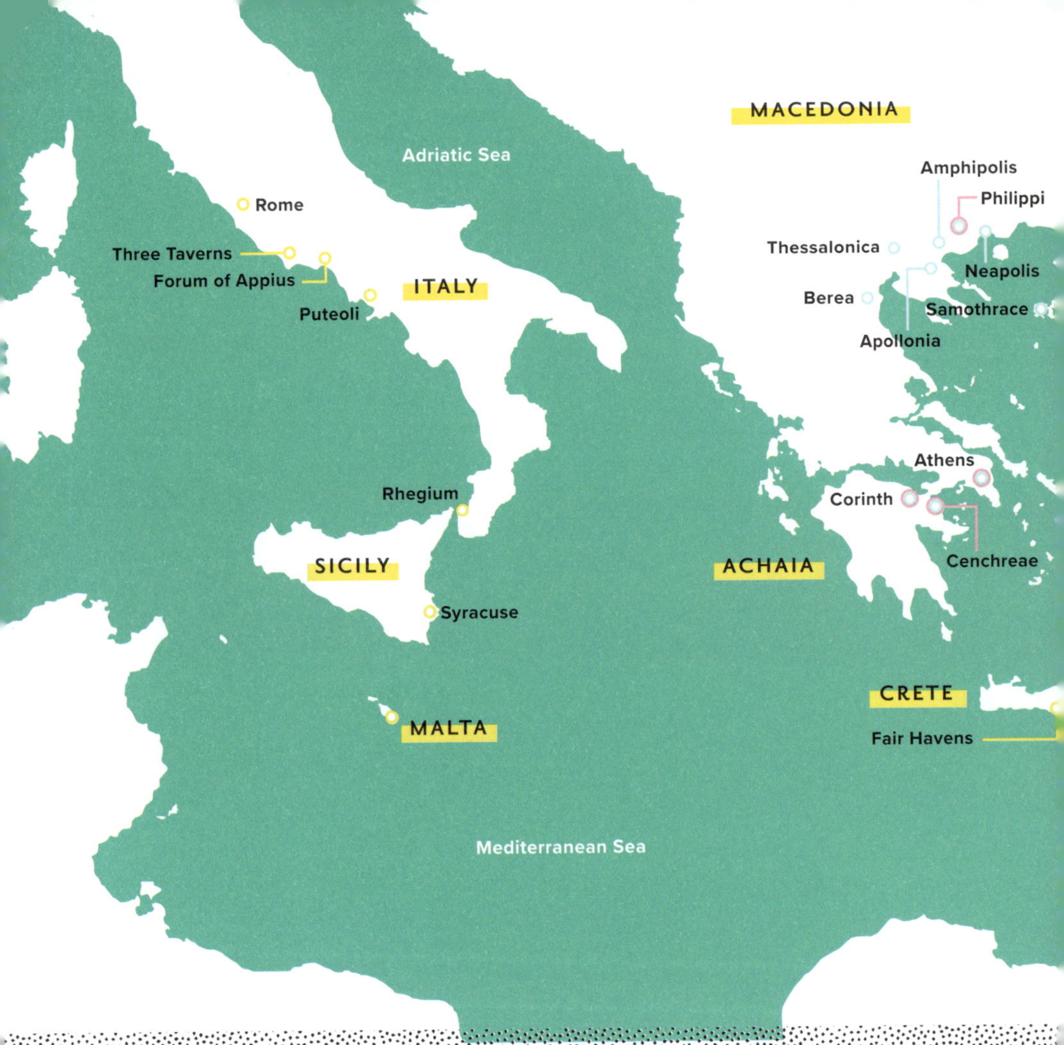
MACEDONIA
Adriatic Sea
Amphipolis
Philippi
Rome
Three Taverns
Thessalonica
Neapolis
Forum of Appius
ITALY
Berea
Samothrace
Puteoli
Apollonia
Athens
Rhegium
Corinth
SICILY
ACHAIA
Cenchreae
Syracuse
CRETE
MALTA
Fair Havens
Mediterranean Sea

PAUL'S MISSIONARY JOURNEYS

The book of Acts begins with Jesus telling His disciples to share the gospel with people "in Jerusalem, in all Judea and Samaria, and to the end of the earth" (1:8). It was Paul and his friends who first took on the challenge of traveling to far-off places to tell people about Jesus. On this map, you can see the places Paul visited, bringing good news to people from every walk of life.

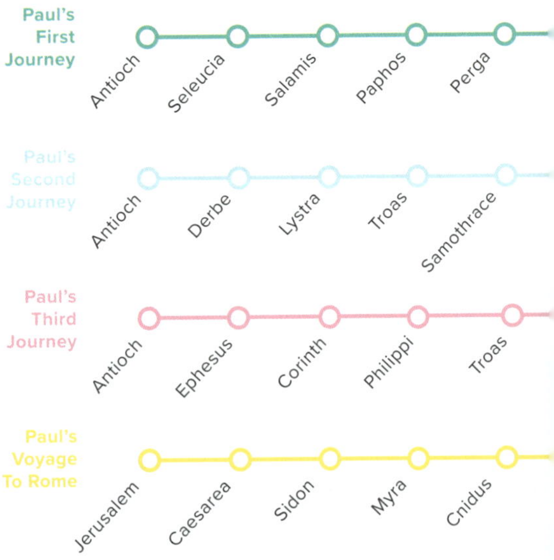
Paul's First Journey
Antioch
Seleucia
Salamis
Paphos
Perga
Paul's Second Journey
Antioch
Derbe
Lystra
Troas
Samothrace
Paul's Third Journey
Antioch
Ephesus
Corinth
Philippi
Troas
Paul's Voyage To Rome
Jerusalem
Caesarea
Sidon
Myra
Cnidus

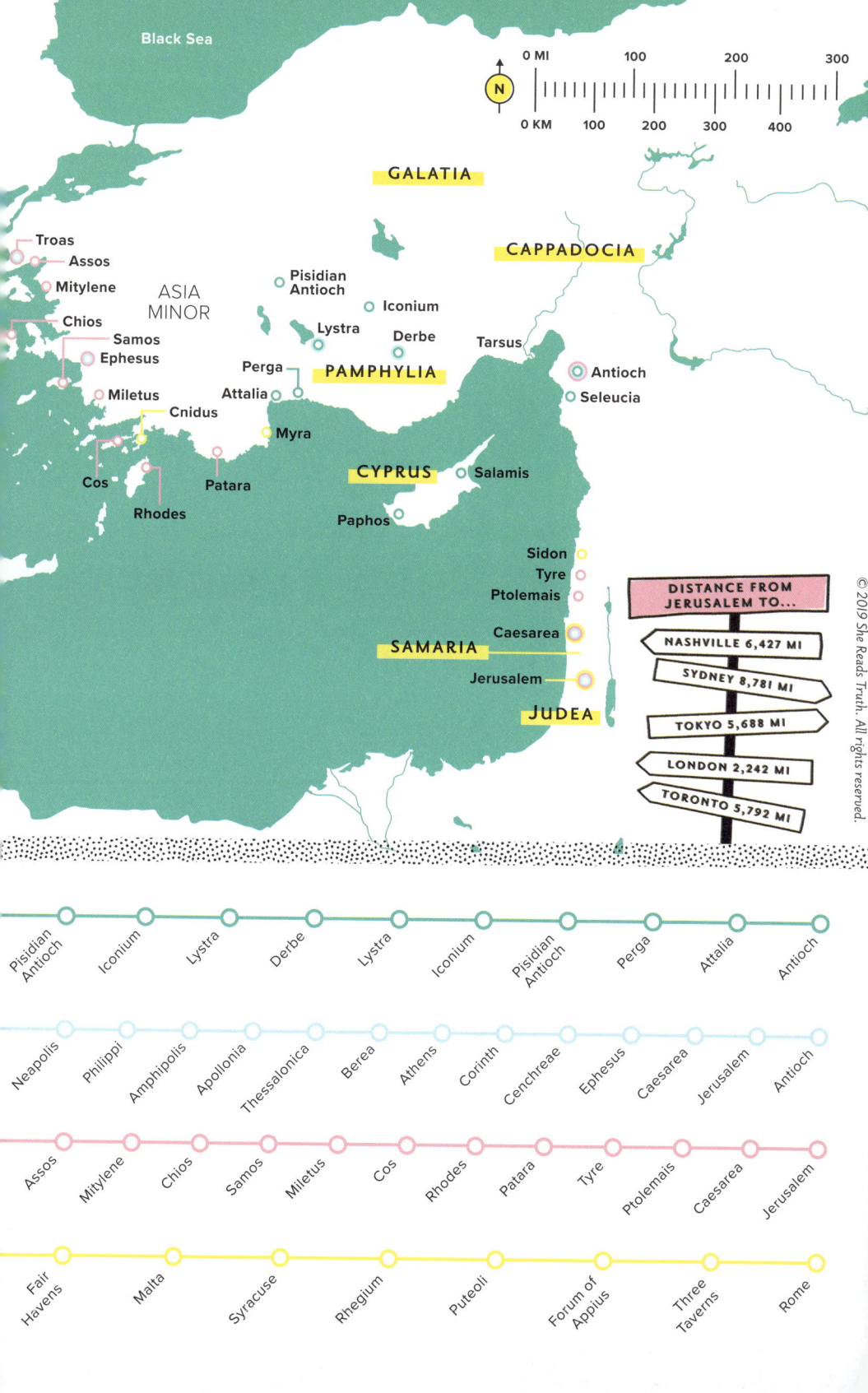

CITY SCRAMBLE

Test your knowledge of the cities Paul visited on his missionary journeys! Unscramble the letters to reveal the answers. Use the map on pages 54–55 if you get stuck.

1. This city was near the Orontes River (Acts 15:22).

_ _ (_) _ _ _ _
H O I N A T C

2. This city was a "free city," which meant that the Roman military didn't have a presence there (Acts 17:1).

_ (_) _ _ _ _ _ _ _ _
A O N S T E H S A I C L

3. Paul had to flee this city when Jewish leaders from Thessalonica came and started a revolt against him (Acts 17:13).

_ _ _ (_) _
E B R A E

4. Paul brought a man named Eutychus (who had fallen out of a window!) back to life in this city (Acts 20:7–12).

_ _ (_) _ _
S R O T A

5. Lydia became a follower of Jesus in this city (Acts 16:11–15).

_ _ _ _ _ (_) _ _
H I L P P P I I

6. In this city, Paul preached in the Areopagus, which was a rocky hill where the city's ruling council met (Acts 17:22).

_ (_) _ _ _ _
S H T E N A

7. Paul met Aquila and Priscilla in this city (Acts 18:1).

_ _ (_) _ _ _ _
T C I N O R H

8. In this city, the people thought Paul and Barnabas were gods (Acts 14:8–13).

(_) _ _ _ _ _
A Y T L S R

9. The Temple of Artemis (one of the Seven Wonders of the Ancient World) was near this city (Acts 19:1).

_ _ _ _ (_) _
S E H U P E S

10. Paul's voyage to Rome started in this city (Acts 21:17).

_ _ _ _ (_) _ _ _
U E A M E L J S R

BONUS Write down the letters in the yellow circles to answer this question: Who is the book of Acts addressed to?

_ _ _ _ _ _ _ _ _ _
1 2 3 4 5 6 7 8 9 10

Answer key on page 80

SHE READS

Read Acts 18
Focus verses:
Acts 18:1–17, 24–28

SHE STUDIES

Take notes as you read.

What happened in the passage?

What was interesting?

Was anything confusing?

POP QUIZ!

What job did Aquila, Priscilla, and Paul have in common?

SHE WONDERS

Date   /   /

This passage names several people who supported and encouraged Paul while he was in Corinth. Who were they? How did they support him?

Later in the passage, two people helped Apollos. Who were they? How did they help him?

Make a list of people who teach, support, and encourage you in your faith. Why are you grateful for each of them?

SHE PRAYS

Talk to God or write Him a note. Take time to pray for the people in your life listed above.

ACTS 19

SHE READS

Read Acts 19
Focus verses:
Acts 19:23–41

SHE STUDIES

Take notes as you read.

What happened in the passage?

What was interesting?

Was anything confusing?

POP QUIZ!

How long did Paul teach at the hall of Tyrannus?

SHE WONDERS

Date   /   /

In this chapter, thousands of people protested Paul's words. Who led this opposition? What was the true cause of his complaint?

What might it cost you to follow Jesus? How does that make you feel?

Look up James 1:2–4 in your Bible. How does it encourage you?

SHE PRAYS

Talk to God or write Him a note. Write a prayer based on James 1:2–4.

ACTS 20

SHE READS

Read Acts 20
Focus verses:
Acts 20:17–38

SHE STUDIES

Take notes as you read.

What happened in the passage?

What was interesting?

Was anything confusing?

POP QUIZ!

Who fell asleep while Paul was teaching?

SHE WONDERS

Date   /   /

Paul said these would be his last words to his friends in Ephesus. What sticks out to you as you read them?

What did Paul want his friends in Ephesus to know?

How did Paul's speech encourage or challenge you?

SHE PRAYS

Talk to God or write Him a note. Thank Him for a specific truth you learned from Paul's speech.

ACTS 21:1-36

SHE READS

Read Acts 21:1–36
Focus verses:
Acts 21:1–16

SHE STUDIES

Take notes as you read.

What happened in the passage?

What was interesting?

Was anything confusing?

POP QUIZ!

What did the prophet Agabus use to tie his hands and feet?

SHE WONDERS

Date   /   /

It was pretty clear what was going to happen to Paul if he went to Jerusalem. Who warned him? How did Paul answer?

Think back through the book of Acts. How would you describe Paul's faith?

In what ways would you like your own faith to grow?

SHE PRAYS

Talk to God or write Him a note. Thank Him for Paul's faith and ask Him to grow yours.

SHE READS

**Acts 21:37–40;
Acts 22; Acts 23:1–11**
Focus verses:
Acts 21:37–40;
Acts 22:22–29

SHE STUDIES

Take notes as you read.

What happened in the passage?

What was interesting?

Was anything confusing?

POP QUIZ!

What language did Paul speak to the Jerusalem mob?

SHE WONDERS

Date   /   /

Paul spoke to two different audiences here: the Jewish crowds and the Roman commander. How were his messages similar? How were they different?

Think about how you would respond if someone asked you what you believe about God. What would you say?

SHE PRAYS

Talk to God or write Him a note. Ask Him for wisdom and courage to talk about your faith with the people in your life who don't know Jesus. (Look back at the list you made on page 49.)

ACTS 23:12–35

SHE READS

Read Acts 23:12–35
Focus verses:
Acts 23:12–35

SHE STUDIES

Take notes as you read.

What happened in the passage?

What was interesting?

Was anything confusing?

As a Roman citizen, Paul had certain rights. Roman citizens could not be beaten and they could request a trial before Caesar.

POP QUIZ!

Which of Paul's relatives visited him in the barracks?

SHE WONDERS

Date   /   /

How did God protect Paul in this story? What people and circumstances did God place in Paul's life to protect him?

Think about Paul's journey in Acts so far. List some of the challenges he faced. How do you see God working in Paul's story?

SHE PRAYS

Talk to God or write Him a note. Ask Him to show you how He is at work in your story.

SHE READS

Read Acts 24
Focus verses:
Acts 24:1–21

SHE STUDIES

Take notes as you read.

What happened in the passage?

What was interesting?

Was anything confusing?

POP QUIZ!

What was the name of Felix's wife?

SHE WONDERS

Date   /   /

Why do you think Paul describes the Christian faith as "the Way" in verse 14?

Where did Paul put his hope?

Paul knew he was in trouble, but he spoke with authority and peace. Do you feel like you have strength and peace in God? Why or why not?

SHE PRAYS

Talk to God or write Him a note. Ask Him to fill you with His strength and peace today.

SHE READS

Read Acts 25; Acts 26
Focus verses:
Acts 26:12–23

SHE STUDIES

Take notes as you read.

What happened in the passage?

What was interesting?

Was anything confusing?

POP QUIZ!
Paul appealed to _____.

SHE WONDERS

Date   /   /

What story did Paul tell in these verses? Why did he share it?

Paul told King Agrippa about his relationship with Jesus. If you could tell one famous person about Jesus, who would it be and why?

Do you have a relationship with Jesus? How would you describe it?

SHE PRAYS

Talk to God or write Him a note. Thank Him for inviting us to have a relationship with Him through Jesus.

SHE READS

**Read Acts 27;
Acts 28:1–10**
Focus verses:
Acts 27:13–38

SHE STUDIES

Take notes as you read.

What happened in
the passage?

What was interesting?

Was anything confusing?

POP QUIZ!

Where was Paul bitten?

SHE WONDERS

Date   /   /

Even though Paul was a prisoner, he was the one who led and encouraged the sailors. Why do you think it turned out that way?

Have you ever been in a situation where you've been the leader or encourager when you didn't expect to be? What happened?

What did Paul do in Acts 27:35? Do you think this surprised the sailors? Why or why not?

SHE PRAYS

Talk to God or write Him a note. Ask him to give you a heart that is thankful even in hard times.

SHE READS

Read Acts 28:11–31
Focus verses:
Acts 28:17–31

SHE STUDIES

Take notes as you read.

What happened in the passage?

What was interesting?

Was anything confusing?

POP QUIZ!

In Rome, Paul lived with _____

SHE WONDERS

Date   /   /

Paul said he was wearing chains for "the hope of Israel." Who is the hope of Israel?

Jesus told His followers to share the gospel "in Jerusalem, in all Judea and Samaria, and to the end of the earth" (Acts 1:8), until everyone hears. At the end of Acts, Paul was telling people about Jesus in Rome, and there's still more work to do today. What role can you play in taking the gospel to everyone who still needs to hear?

SHE PRAYS

Talk to God or write Him a note. Thank Him for the book of Acts!

FOR THE RECORD

WHILE I WAS READING ACTS...

THIS IS WHERE I READ:

- Home
- School
- Church
- Coffee shop
- A friend's house
- Other

I WAS LISTENING TO:

Artist:

Song:

Playlist:

I WAS WATCHING:

Shows:

Movies:

THIS IS WHEN I READ:

- In the morning
- In the afternoon
- At night

MY FAVORITE SUBJECT IN SCHOOL:

MY FAVORITE HOBBIES:

WHAT WAS HAPPENING IN THE WORLD:

WHAT WAS HAPPENING IN MY LIFE:

WHAT I AM LOOKING FORWARD TO:

CROSSWORD PUZZLE
(Page 33)

1. Philip
2. Barnabas
3. Matthias
4. Theophilus
5. Peter
6. Priscilla
7. Paul or Saul
8. Cornelius
9. Lydia
10. Dorcas

CITY SCRAMBLE
(Page 57)

1. Antioch
2. Thessalonica
3. Berea
4. Corinth
5. Philippi
6. Athens
7. Ephesus
8. Lystra
9. Troas
10. Jerusalem

Bonus: Theophilus